MW01032430

THE HITTITES

A History from Beginning to End

Copyright © 2016 by Hourly History.

All rights reserved.

Table of Contents

Introduction

The past intrigues our study of ancient human empires as we look for common threads and differences in the world we live in today. By studying past cultures we can better understand humankind and piece together our collective human experience. The Hittites, who were said to have lived among gods and kings, were mysterious enough to captivate even Lawrence of Arabia. Vast inquiries into their civilization have formed the basis for extensive research gleaned from analyzing historical and archaeological information that looks to Hittite clay tablets to unearth a plausible prototype for Homer's Helen of Troy. These Indo-European Hittites settled in what would become modern day Turkey and Syria and developed a civilization that was a power to be reckoned with—one that profoundly impacted the superpowers of their time and those that immediately followed. Thanks to their tradition of preservation and meticulous record-keeping, the Hittites left us with an immense amount of documentation that provides us a window into our shared past that might have remained shaky if left only to speculation, or worse remained obscured.

Through the sands of time, the Hittites have been revealed to have been cosmopolitan and devoted to becoming one of the greatest empires of all time. They throned great kings that ruled among the empires of Egypt, Babylonia and Assyria. They savagely attacked ancient Babylonia only to later hold key evidence in their magnificent excavated libraries that preserved Babylonian works from humankind's early thinkers. Their penchant for storing knowledge revealed their role in preserving customs and traditions of sophisticated Eastern cultures to the West for our shared human interest in preservation. While they are often known for their extremely disciplined tactics in times of war, they are similarly understood through further research to have shown an immensely unprecedented understanding for developing sensitivity as well as moral and ethical insights, as indicated in their reformation of laws, skilled international relations, and their written records.

These ritualistic tradition-preserving multilingual people that took oaths very seriously conquered and invaded many lands. The mysteries that surround their human struggle for power, wealth, understanding of cosmic and socio-political order, and dominion include probable cultural and political ties to the land of Troy and deepen our understanding of the precursors of ancient Greek contributions to our human advancements. Those who dared venture into Hittite territory encountered worthy opponents skilled in the art of war and diplomacy, equally at ease with conducting embargoes and raids for both conquest and peace. The great Egypt, during an era of unprecedented power and wealth, had a Hittite problem. Their wartime efforts secured for them vast resources, but also led to meaningful "brotherly" relations with the key players of the region. They were legendary, significant and meticulous.

The Hittites lived in a time when heroes and heroines of ancient civilizations could take actions that could direct entire civilizations. They asserted their ambition to be an international power and in the process have left our human story a rich treasure trove of their complex civilization as it related to the three superpowers of the time. For 3000 years, while the Hittites were the unknown fourth empire that held power between 1800 and 1200 BCE, their influence and their complex system of collective governance—seen as an early example of early Middle

Eastern democracy that did not give a king absolute power in decision-making—guides us in gaining informed insight into their strengths, weaknesses, achievements, and what destabilized them and eventually led to their ruin.

Chapter One

Sources

In the early 1880s, the Reverend Archibald Henry Sayce and William Wright pioneered the idea that there might be another empire the world had overlooked. They conjectured that it was considered as great as the empires of Egypt, Babylonia and Assyria during the second millennium BCE. Sayce, the British clergyman who first disclosed the Hittites mentioned in the Bible to the world of scholarship, was also a premier Assyriologist and linguist, and held a chair as Professor of Assyriology at the University of Oxford. His colleague William Wright, a missionary and an author, conducted investigations while in Syria that led him to conclude that the casts he made of inscriptions that were found were in fact Hittite remains, and that a Hittite empire had at one time existed in Asia Minor and Northern Syria. Sayce had come to similar conclusions in his work.

The distribution of monuments inscribed with a distinctive form of hieroglyphic writing that looked different than known types of writing led them toward their conclusion. Upon review of cuneiform clay tablets from the 14th Century BCE found in Amarna archives, they also noticed that Egyptian kings corresponded with Hittite kings as if they had been seen as equals. Although the earliest expeditions to the area occurred in 1834 by explorer Charles Texier, their publications on the possibility of the Hittites drew attention. Hieroglyphic texts at various sites in the Taurus Mountains, Cilicia, and northern Syrian principalities flourished from the beginning of the 12th century BCE until the end of the 8th century BCE. These texts led scholars of the 19th century to postulate the existence of the Hittite Empire in the first place, although most of these texts had been actually written after their capital Hattusa had been destroyed. They were in a Luwian dialect, an unsolved mystery that the infamous Lawrence of Arabia was tasked in helping renowned British archaeologist David Hogarth unravel. (His work will be discussed in the next chapter.)

Finally, in 1906, Hugo Winckler, an expert in ancient Near Eastern languages, and Theodor Makridi, an Ottoman archaeologist, discovered the royal archives of the Hittite Empire in modern-day Boğazköy, which was formerly Hattusa, the capital of the Hittite Empire. There they found a flood of documentary evidence that revolutionized our comprehension of who the Hittites were and the role they played in the world of the second millennium BCE. They found two major archives filled with thousands of tablets and fragments.

As opposed to other archaeological digs focused on ancient civilizations, these weren't commonplace commercial documents either. These were characterized as intellectual tools required for the political and ideological maintenance of their empire. The 1906 expedition yielded 30,000-35,000 texts and fragments representing about 3,000-3,500 original tablets. They include treaties, royal correspondences, prayers, rituals, festival descriptions, myths, literature, and laws.

While this turn of events marked a huge discovery, the archaeologists weren't the only ones now ready to decipher their written record as well as other artifacts. Philologists have been studying Hittites as students of ancient languages. Linguists attempt to reassemble the components of the family of languages to which they belong. Historians study the royal annals and other texts that help them establish the Hittite presence in the world history books. Anthropologists look at the aspects of their society that would interest us. Geologists and other earth science experts consider their natural resources and environment. Plenty of evidence compels art historians, given the number of seal impressions and rock-cut reliefs found, and there's a lot to debate about for ancient technology students and archaeologists.

Although tablets and seal impressions have been found in other locations, when experts evaluate the sources of information that have helped piece together the lives of the Hittites, they find some fascinating revelations. Many of the historical works written by the Hittites were primarily works of royal propaganda, according to Professor Henry Hoffner, a notable Assyriologist and Hittotologist and the Executive Editor of the Chicago Hittite Dictionary. Often, their scribes presented a picture of a kingdom geared for chronic warfare, since rulers emphasized military successes in the records. Their official records presented only their public face: there were never any bad rulers and they documented no criticism. Very diplomatic, and we'll see how central formality and diplomacy were to administrative aspects of their lives in the following pages. Instead, they blamed circumstances beyond their control rather than lack of ability or missteps on the part of their leaders. Kings were cut off from their subjects and many of these official records screen readers from their private lives, idiosyncrasies and defects.

However, this is obviously not the full picture. A majority of the texts have nothing to do with the military side of Hittite life and provide a more balanced view of life and society. The archived tablets are in no fewer than eight languages. There are testaments that record kings' speeches and provide rare glimpses into the actual personalities and emotions of Hittite kings, appeals from Egyptian wives to Hittite kings in times of great tragedy, descriptions of strict conditions of hygiene that kept subjects far from kings and their nearest relations, duties and regulations for reporting officials on day-to-day operations in the service of the king, as well as proclamations and various reports.

According to leading expert Gary Chapman, there are practically no records of non-elite residents of the Hatti, the name the Hittites used for their homelands. Experts have read about the use and abuse of receipts and trade negotiations; however, none of these documents has been recovered. One possibility is that these were written on perishable material, since there is evidence of a perishable class of documentation that played a large role in Hittite administration. Cuneiform clay tablets appear to be used only in the service of royal establishment and since they used both wood and clay tablets, the existence of Hittite ephemera is possible.

Piecing all of these together, we start to see a fuller picture. In collecting this information from the leading experts and authors on Hittites, we present to you the following chapters in an attempt to broaden your understanding of the place-marker that almost left a gaping hole in our understanding of our ancient past.

Chapter Two

Lawrence of Arabia, Helen of Troy, Origins and Remarkable Missing Links

In our contemporary times, ancient monuments in Syria and Iraq are under continual attack by members of the so-called Islamic State, extremist groups, and those embroiled civil wars. However, specific sites in the region were once primary centers of life, power and trade for the Hittites. They have been explored by some of humanity's most eager minds, including Lawrence of Arabia. He was known as T.E. Lawrence during his time. Sponsored by the British Museum, a very young 20-year-old Lawrence of Arabia, studying Middle Eastern architecture at Oxford University, was passionate about medieval epics and conducted a thesis to prove that the Western architecture of the Crusaders was inspired by Eastern influences. This work led him to Syria in 1909.

His extraordinary studies caught the attention of renowned British archaeologist David Hogarth, who sat on the board of the Royal Geographic Society. He asked Lawrence to return from Syria with ancient Hittite seals that piqued the archaeologist's interest. Lawrence didn't fail. He brought back thirty rare artifacts. This impressed Hogarth, who then hired Lawrence to work on an archaeological dig at the ancient city of Carchemish, a Hittite ruin located on the latter-day Syria-Turkish border. It was a provincial capital dating from as early as 2500

BCE, which had been discovered in 1876 by British scholars.

Hogarth wanted to uncover the secret of Hittite hieroglyphics and was on the elusive trail of a word key that would help him achieve his mission. Lawrence arrived in Carchemish in the spring of 1911 and worked with archaeologist Leonard Woolley. From 1911 to 1914, preceding World War I, Lawrence led many of the digs and was later knighted as a tribute to his distinguished archaeological career. He developed a remarkable rapport with the 200-300 Arab and Kurdish workers, treating them as equals, and as he absorbed their culture, he also developed a better understanding of their long-standing feuds, aspirations and religions.

His expedition in March 1914 became a Scientific American Supplement and shared some of the mystery surrounding the royal city in Carchemish with those interested in the world. Hogarth would prove to be a lifelong mentor to Lawrence, which led to Lawrence's intelligence career with the British forces in the Middle East after the war broke out and all excavations ceased. Lawrence and Hogarth's epic digs threw new light on the vast scale of the ring-walled fortified city enclosures that had once contained palaces, citadels, commons quarters, open courts, lion-guarded portals, and higher quality sculptures and art than was previously found.

In early 2014, the Islamic State hung its black flag over Jarablus, the current name of Carchemish in Syria. However, the site was still opened to the public for the first time for nearly a century, despite being partly under the control of IS jihadists. Carchemish was an important site during the many scenes of battles over the millennia between Egyptians, Assyrians, Babylonians and Hittites. Carchemish captured the world's imagination, including the devotion of Lawrence of Arabia. Popular books explain his adventures and impactful relations that helped bring insight into this ancient Hittite city and the dynastic ambitions among those who warred and traded in the Middle East.

If the Hittites were just as driven by ambition to dominate in the lands of the Middle East as their neighboring empires, then how did these Indo-European people emerge in these ancient lands? It is believed by some experts that the original Hittites migrated from beyond the Black Sea from the area which is now Bulgaria and Ukraine. Unlike other ancient civilizations, the Hittites did not necessarily establish city-states or tribally-controlled territories. Historians agree on the absence of city-states during the Hittite period. While history considered the Hittites may have been a small Canaanite tribe that dwelt in the Palestinian hills, they were discovered to have built a great empire from the Aegean Sea's eastern shores to the banks of the Euphrates. They ruled over a network of vassal states and developed local autonomy.

While much scholarly work describes the Hittites as originally Indo-European, there is also a lot of evidence that suggests the Hittites that established themselves in Anatolia didn't have a single common ethnic core, or a single common language. Instead, they were multiracial in character and spoke a number of different languages during the course of their empire building. While Hittite (or as they called it, Nesite) is considered among the oldest recorded Indo-European languages, expert Gary Beckman reported that eight different languages were found in documents from Hattusa. While most of them were in Hittite, they were also in Semitic Akkadian, Hattic, Palaic, Luwian, Hurrian, Sumerian, and Indic.

Did the Hittites possibly inspire the story of Helen of Troy and what brought them in contact with the people of Troy, given that the Hittite empire was around during the supposed Trojan Wars? The city of Troy (Ilios) was part of an entity known as Wilusa on the fringes of the influential Hittite empire. Documentary evidence attests to friendly diplomatic and wartime relations between the Trojan and Hittite authorities from the mid-13th century BCE. There are striking similarities between Troy's kingdom and their other great settlements within the Hittite empire. Since the Hittites kept meticulous written records and little evidence has emerged from Troy, some relevant discoveries have emerged that tie into the story of Helen of Troy and the Trojan prince Paris during the supposed Trojan Wars.

In 2014, it emerged that a tablet referred to as tablet CTH 183 written in the Hittite language utilizing the cuneiform script was a letter commissioned by a Mycenaean Greek king and sent to a Hittite king (most likely Muwatalli II who reigned ca 1295-1272 BCE) over the rightful ownership of a group of islands off of the Anatolian coast that had formed a part of a dowry in a previous generation. The diplomatic marriage of the Mycenaean king to an unknown Assuwan princess was the reason that the Assuwa people had given the lands in question as part of her marriage dowry to the king. Archaeologists and historians find it plausible that this unknown Assuwan princess is the prototype for Homer's Helen, the heart of countless legends and the basis for extensive research on the links between Homer's Trojan Wars and the Hittite empire.

As experts piece together the potential alliances and inter-relations between the legendary figures depicted in Homer's Trojan Wars, we continue to marvel at questions as further research builds. Archival analysis has yielded breakthroughs in identifying specific events in the archaeological Hittite records that correspond directly to Homer's Trojan War. The war supposedly took place around the time of the end of the Hittite empire and the

Mycenaean civilization of Greece collapsed. Professor David Hawkins of the School of Oriental and African Studies in London made an important breakthrough in 1997 based on an inscription associated with a sculpture, in conjunction with a letter written by King Manapa-Tarhunda of the Seha River Land to his Hittite overlord. They were able to locate the kingdom of Wilusa. Several key scholars now believe that Wilusa and Troy are one and the same, bringing the almost one-hundred-year search for references to Troy in the Hittite tablets closer to an answer. More research seems to suggest that the Trojans spoke a language close to Hittite, Luwian, and that correspondences reveal that they corresponded with the Hittite king at the time.

Since Troy was an outpost of the Hittite world, it commanded a position on the trade routes of the northern Aegean Sea and became desirable. Who should exercise influence over Wilusa was the subject of correspondences between the Hittite ruler and the king of Ahhiyawa. There is some possibility that the Trojan Wars were not between great kings, but low-level endemic conflicts between ambitious mercenary captains that were loyal to their own ethnic groups, but that at some point the Hittites did have to assert their dominion over the area. Troy risked drawing the attention of greedy conquerors because of its attractive geopolitical position on the trade routes running from the Mediterranean into Anatolia.

Ongoing studies reveal that there were Hittite goods found in Troy and that the first likely mention of Troy comes from the record of a military expedition conducted by the Hittite king Tudhaliya against the Confederacy of Assuwa in the late 15th century BCE, when he restored a deposed king of Wilusa. Even under the previous king, Muwatalli, Wilusa was highly-prized. Although it held unswerving loyalty to the Hittites, several attacks on its land, as well as other vassal states, led to treaties between the Hittites and Troy creating a required allegiance and spelled out Troy's requirement to lend military assistance to Hittites on campaigns. There is much discussion on the Iliad, within the context of the Hittite empire, and the contact between the Trojans and the Hittites that is worth exploring that you can find in the Further Reading section at the end of this primer.

It is fortunate for us that Lawrence of Arabia and modern enthusiasts continue to shine a light on the mysterious Hittites and also debate the historical basis of the Iliad for centuries. In the pages that follow, we'll take you on a quick journey into some of the prevalent aspects of the world of the Hittites and how their preservation of ancient history made our studies and interpretations of the time when they walked the earth among gods and kings possible, as we yearn to piece together our connection to our shared past.

Chapter Three

The Bronze and Iron Age – Hittites and their Contemporaries

At the dawn of the Late Bronze Age, during the second millennium BCE, the Hittites were bent on world domination. They built their capital Hattusa in a remote location, miles away from any major river or the sea. They arose in what is now modern day Turkey in central Anatolia and became a superpower of the ancient Near Eastern world, building their kingdom of Hatti to be a powerful empire fueled by order, fear and the desire for expansion. Theirs was a life based on duty, discipline and sacrifice. They built their city out of the granite mountains of the North-Central Anatolian Mountain Range, using the natural landscape to build a thick wall along sheer cliffs to secure their city, home to more than 50,000. Their brutal army and their ambitions helped them build an empire that rivaled Egypt and Babylon. Their armies stretched their vast empire westward across Anatolia to the Aegean Sea, south eastwards through northern Syria, and then across the Euphrates River into the western fringes of Mesopotamia.

During their formative years in the 18th and 17th centuries BCE, the Hittites bent the natural landscape to their will in order to fit their needs. Archaeologists commonly divide Hittite history into Old Kingdom (up until 1400 BCE) and New Kingdom (circa 1400-early 12th century BCE). Their fortress city was enclosed in a wall over five miles long and is considered among the thickest walls in the ancient world. Dr. Andreas Schachner from the German Archaeological Institute found that these large walls had compartments and were a mix of earth and sand; they were set like concrete. Every twelve meters, they built a watchtower. Their gateways were traps for any enemy who dared to enter without invitation and they built secret tunnels in an inner wall within the fortress for the purpose of ambushing anyone who might have gotten past the first wall; Hittite soldiers could also use these passages to leave in secret during an attack or occupation. They devised a groundwater management system that was ahead of their time, where they piped in natural springs from the hills above their city and ran the water into seven storage pools within the city walls.

The Hittite Kingdom accomplished a great deal during the middle Bronze Age and subsequent Iron Age. They made full use of Anatolia's mineral wealth and nearby territories. The silver-rich Hittites made animal figurines that date back to the 3rd millennium BCE. They were the first in history to mine, smelt and utilize iron from the region of present day Armenia in order to craft tools and weapons. Their means of refinement made iron stronger, which secured them a great advantage in warfare as a Mesopotamian civilization, cutting through the copper swords and shields of their enemies. Following their invention of tempering, iron came to widespread use and was highly prized for use in weaponry and in farm equipment. One of the tribes subject to Hittite rule, the Chalybes, were the first people to make steel in approximately 1400 BCE.

Anatolia also had rich deposits of a number of other metals, including copper, silver, and gold. It attracted Assyrian merchants who brought tin and textiles to trade for this ore. Commerce flourished throughout their empire and was protected by the authorities and standing army.

The medium of exchange in trade was silver, which was measured by weight. The unit of weight was the shekel. With the origin of the use of iron, the Hittites influenced the world forever and changed the metallurgy of the ancient world. However, it is interesting to note that the Hittites did not share their knowledge of iron with their own farmers, because they did not trust them but instead feared them, seeing them as potential rebels. Still, they were willing to export their weapons as prized items in trade. They withheld knowledge of how iron was made.

As soon as they gained control of the Mesopotamian region, the Hittites began to trade. However, there were long-established trade routes, preceding the Old Assyrian colonies in Anatolia, which ran from the Mediterranean northward through central Anatolia and onward to the Black Sea outlets, so that ships could reach Troy and beyond. Textiles were a significant part of trade during the 3rd millennium BCE. They established trade relations with Egypt, Mycenaeans, Babylon, Greece, the Mittanis and the Levant (the eastern Mediterranean coastal lands of Asia Minor and Phoenicia, which is modern-day Turkey, Syria, and Lebanon). The Hittites operated complex trade operations and their enterprises were often privately-owned. In the 16th century BCE, they seized trade routes in Syria and the Levant, actions which were contested by Egypt and the Mitanni.

These lucrative trade routes fell into their hands and control of trade and natural resources in the region between Greece, Egypt and the Levant were at stake as they challenged Egypt for control of Syria and Palestine. They wanted to control all of the trade routes and metal sources, and much has been written about their struggle to control these routes as a means to gain hegemony in the region. As the Hittite empire expanded southward and the Egyptian empire expanded northeastward, the stakes were raised even higher. The Levant and especially Syria were at stake. Egyptians depended on Syria as a place of trade with India, which was a great source of wealth for them. Syria's importance during ancient times cannot be underestimated, since it became the meeting place of ancient empires given its geographical position. Egypt's Pharaohs were anxious to retain their hold on trade by Syrian land routes, since it was considerable. The clash of interests resulted in a great chariot battle at Kadesh (Qadesh) around 1275 BCE. Much has been written about this famous battle and the results, implications, and significant contribution to human history will be explored in the pages that follow.

Suffice it to say, Near East trade had various middlemen that were crucial for various trade partners, revealing that Syria and the areas of conflict that we see in the news daily aren't simply contemporary, but instead locations that have seen historical levels of strife. These regions include Syria, where modern commercial centers like Aleppo, Damascus, Beirut and other cities became carriers of the trade of the Persian Gulf to the Mediterranean lands. When the lure of India was brought to the Mediterranean world, the conflicting interests of those empires, like the Hittites', could bring on the conditions of war, which put the Hittites and Egypt at loggerheads.

International trade between the Aegean civilizations and the Egyptians, Hittites, and Babylonians developed along these sea and land routes, despite near-constant warfare and constantly shifting alliances. These civilizations all widened their spheres of trade and influence. While much of Egyptian trade moved by water routes, Hittites and Babylonians conducted trade by caravan. It is formidable that the ancient Hittite empire, located in the region of Anatolia, Syria and ancient Phoenicia, controlled the trade routes between Greece, Egypt and Babylon.

Artifacts and seals reveal an extensive trade network existed within the empire. Israelites acted as intermediaries in trade between Egyptians and Hittites. According to the world-renowned expert Sayce, the city of Carchemish, a viceregal kingdom of the Hittites and as previously described the site where Lawrence of Arabia extracted relics, was the center of overland trade in Western Asia. It brought products of Phoenicia and the West to the civilized populations of Assyria and Babylon. Israelites exported horses and chariots from Egypt into Carchemish, where markets for foreign goods were held regularly. It appears then that Hittite international trade was more limited in comparison to other ancient empires since the Hittites relied heavily on simply conquering areas that produced goods that they wanted. They had a loan and credit system that operated widely in Eastern Anatolia where rates of interest were high, ranging from 30% to as much as 180%. Local kings had to resolve problems by issuing decrees cancelling all debts, since indebtedness grew to become a big problem.

As mentioned, the Hittites came to play a serious role in the history of Egypt and in the process became recognized as a great power. They influenced the principalities of the Aegean coast, down the Euphrates and across Syria. The Kaska to the north, who inhabited the Pontic Mountains of Anatolia, were called swine herders and weavers of linen in Hittite texts. They were an enemy threat and one that was a particular menace throughout the time of their empire. The Hittites conquered the area called Cilicia by the Greeks, which was located to the southeast of their territory. However, this region would later fall under the influence of the Syrian Mittanis, then achieved independence as Kizzuwatna and was absorbed by Hatti in the mid-14th century BCE. Hatti also extended its rule beyond the Taurus Mountains into Northern Syria initially in the late

17th century. They broke the power of Yamhad, the Amorite kingdom centered in Aleppo, and put an end to their system of independent city-states. Aleppo was one of the earliest threats to Hittite ambitions and had once actually cut the Hittites off from the rich trade of Syria.

Warfare was both an economic and political necessity of their times. Their invasion of Babylon was notorious and will be further discussed in the following chapters, as will their wars and diplomatic relations with the ruling empires of the time. The kingdom exhibited influence on many people and territories.

The nature of their relationships with their contemporaries was complex. Egypt, Mitannis and Hittites competed directly in the coastal zone and they shared complex dealings on all frontiers. Since Hittites were diplomatic players, they rose to power by melding conquest and astute political maneuvering. They referred to the Mycenaean region as Ahhiyawa. Although there is evidence of relations between them and the Hittites, it is notable that the rulers of Egypt, Babylon, Assyria and the Hittites formed an elite highly exclusive club and addressed each other as brothers, despite the underlying tensions and distrust that erupted into open conflicts when their interests crossed.

The Hittites dominated what is now central Turkey politically and militarily for most of the second millennium BCE, but they didn't isolate themselves, despite their remote location. They built their cities and their great empire on military campaigns against the Egyptians and other rivals that led to one of the first international systems between empires. They often found themselves fighting for territorial control of Canaanite states, but also found themselves conducting trade, diplomacy and peace under certain conditions. In fact, the Hittites are considered to have developed the first system of diplomacy and since they were prone to contemplate treaties and peace under certain conditions, their ideas surrounding international relations are considered remarkable by experts.

Although some study has been conducted to understand the extent of influence by Ancient Eastern empires like the Hittites on the origins of abstract thought and philosophy, it is notable to highlight the smooth operation of the Hittites' international relations system, especially in early political development. They did indeed develop international rules, recognizing those empires that were considered equals, and developed a means to clarify their relationships with the surrounding world into a legal order. Besides allies, they had enemies as well as entered into vassalage and protectorate relationships. Their laws of war were also characterized, by comparison to other Ancient Eastern empires, as showing a respect for legalities and human usage. While some depictions have shown the fierceness of this warlike people, it's important to also understand that they also typically instituted a submission at the place of conflict to a besieged town to allow them to preserve the town from destruction and its inhabitants from being taken as captives.

Chapter Four

Life and Times of the Hittites and Notable Events: Kingdoms and Empire-Building

Detailed records reveal that the Hittites' greater purpose was to impose their power on the world. While historians explain that the perception of the Hittites has been that they were a people known as the Hittim in the Old Testament and as the Hetheen in the Greek translation of the Bible - with most of what was known about them contained in the Bible long before modern discoveries - others have focused on piecing together who they were based on their historical record and artifacts as the Hatti and in Egyptian records as Ht'. Their obedience through oaths to their gods forced them to create a system where the oath to kings was most important. The ruling elite executed the king's will. Their sacred bond with each other was a unity of service to the king and it was not the kind of unity that could be broken. They burned effigies of their enemies and designed monuments as evidence of strength and power. The enormity of the architecture that has been found in their vast capital of Hattusa and their other cities stand as remarkable testimony to the attitude they held about how they could grow and fulfill their empire's vision. Anger of their gods could be inflicted on a person and could be enforced by rituals. They developed an unstoppable war machine to create ruthless, disciplined warriors and revolutionized warfare. If a soldier missed a target, there was severe punishment; the training for Hittite troops was constant and absolute.

While we will discuss their complex system of gods and how they lived their lives despite their prevalent political ambitions in a moment, let's first consider what they looked like, the Hittite world view, how the kings ruled and what the responsibilities of the king's subjects were, and then how they cultivated their culture through literature, sports and art. Then, we will briefly look at their economy and return to the earlier discussion about how their imperialism fit in with the different empires nearby while they reached their zenith and ended up ultimately collapsing despite their earlier power.

Their Style

Based on studies conducted by the well-respected Sayce that look at rock wall carvings of musicians, artists, warriors, farmers, kings and everyday people, and on analysis of their written record, scholars have determined what early Hittite men and women dressed and looked like. They were Indo-European and generally had yellow skin and black hair and eyes, with a protrusive nose and square, prominent cheekbones. They wore two different types of head coverings. One was a close-fitted skull-cap; the other, a lofty tiara that was generally pointed, but sometimes rounded at the top or ornamented. They wore snow-shoes or moccasins. The tiaras often featured some embroidery. Women's robes descended to their feet as did the long-sleeved garments of the priests. Men wore tunics, which left their knees bare, but were fastened around the waist by a girdle. They threw a cloak over these items.

They were usually armed and carried a dirk (a long thrusting dagger) in their girdle and a spear and a bow slung over their backs. Their weapons were either bronze or iron and may also have included the battle ax in areas of the Aegean Sea. Their clothing was dyed with various colors and ornamented with fringes and rich designs. Based on observations made by Hripsime Haroutunian in his essay "Bearded or Beardless? Some Speculation on the Function of the Beard among the Hittites" in "Recent Developments in Hittite Archaeology and History: Papers in Memory of Hans G. Guterbock," it is possible to conclude that the Hittites and most of the images of their deities were beardless, except for the supreme god of the Hittite religious pantheon, the weather-god, who wore a beard. In that case, facial hair would have represented manliness, virility, and power for the supreme god.

They were of mixed ethnic origin: Indo-European, native Hattian, Hurrian, Luwian and other ethnicities. Some scholars claim that their mixed population, augmented by repeated arrivals of deportees and prisoners of war, made it so that the government could no longer rely on its subjects' loyalty in the face of enemy incursions. Their official language was called Nesite since they originated in the city of Nesa when it was part of the Assyrian Colony period, and the leaders of this Indo-European group gained control over large parts of the eastern half of Anatolia a century or so before the emergence of the Hittite kingdom.

Their Views

For the Hittites, the course of human events was determined by their gods in accordance with their own principles of justice. For instance, an epidemic could be a form of punishment for a murder committed on behalf of one of their heralded kings Suppiluliuma; conversely, success came to a king like Hattusili III in his bid for the throne because the gods judged his position was stronger than his nephew's. Calamities were the result of divine displeasure with human misdeeds. They were often very consumed with misfortunes. The universe and powers that shaped the weather had a cosmic order, with the sun foremost in the pantheon, although the sun was later displaced by the god of weather and storm. Harvest was secured by appointed prayers and rituals. Omens were consulted before battles and appropriate rituals were performed. These could make the difference for their military campaign. They are credited with certain attitudes that bring them a fraction closer to modern ideals: women were in some respects better treated than elsewhere in the 2nd millennium BCE; capital punishment was restricted to a minority of crimes and offenses against the moral code; although slavery was widespread, it was not entirely oppressive either.

Walking Among Kings

Kings were tripartite rulers. They were priests on behalf of the gods and goddesses, they were the commanders-in-chief of the military, and they were also the highest authority in administrative and judicial matters. Administratively, the king was involved in the affairs and daily activities of the kingdom. He received daily direct reports from high ranking military and administrative officers. Documents that have been unearthed show the daily duties and regulations of these reporting officials.

Most documents tell the story of kings that were not easily accessible neither by those in the service to them or those who he ruled over. However, a testament which recorded King Hattusili's speech gave a rare glimpse into the actual personality, character and emotions of a Hittite king. He has a more human countenance and the text highlighted the personal feelings on the part of the king. In another example, when the infamous king Suppiluliuma, one of the most world-renowned kings of the Hittite empire, received an appeal from the Egyptian Pharaoh Tutankhamun's young widow, he seems nonplussed in his scribe's recording despite the death of the Pharaoh, the brotherhood between the empires, and the fact that the king of the Hittites would understand that since the Pharaoh had not produced an heir, Egypt could become weak. The Egyptian Queen pleaded with the Hittite king in an effort to restore stability to the throne and to the kingdom, exhorting him to bring a lasting alliance by sending one of his sons to become her husband. She reveals her fear for her kingdom and the royal line.

In his quest to figure out whether this was a real appeal or a matter of deceiving him, he sent a chamberlain to go to Egypt and bring back the truth. However, in King Suppiluliuma's biography, which was written by his son Mursili II, he refers to the dead Pharaoh with the Hittite representation of the Pharaoh's name Nibhuriya and his son recorded Suppiluliuma's response, "Such a thing has never happened to me in my whole life!" It was not until the Egyptian Queen sent a second appeal that she reproached the King for sending a chamberlain for fact-gathering given the circumstances. In the end, months later, the Hittite king did send one of his sons, the Hittite Prince Zannanza, who was killed by an Egyptian hit squad as he entered Egypt. An elder courtier named Aye became the Pharaoh of Egypt. There are such glimpses in the annals and in correspondences of kings beyond the image that was sold to their people and to the world that experts continue to study. Through correspondences, we have learned that the great Pharaoh Rameses II described that the Hittite King Suppiluliuma's wife—who was an imported spouse, but a great source of strength to her husband--was held with much esteem internationally and even by Rameses himself.

The monarch was also titled "My Sun-god", designated such as the intersection of the divine sphere with humans. The king was allotted the paramount position in society by the leading deities themselves, and he held sway over large territories that extended over much of Anatolia, into Syria and as far south as Damascus. Since local rulers controlled vassal and protectorate states and were bound by treaty to Hittite overlords, many treaties have survived. In return to their obligations to the Hittite empire, the Hittite King guaranteed support and military assistance. A member of the Hittite royal family ruled each viceregal kingdom. Hittite queens and mothers often had considerable power and played memorable roles in state affairs.

The Hittite Law code was composed during the Old Kingdom and modified during the same period. They were much like the notable Code of Hammurabi, except they were not as harsh in punishment. Instead of an eye for an eye mentality, they allowed people to make payments called compensation to the injured persons. A collection of roughly 200 Hittite laws was found among the tablets discovered in the capital in 1905 and are a single work in 2 tablets, containing laws of different periods. They showed a constant development toward milder and more humane punishment. Their list of offenses with prescribed punishments included homicide, bodily injury, matrimony, private property, sexual taboos, witchcraft and other matters.

Kings were often involved in military campaigns since prowess in war was an essential part of the ideology of kingship. They thus needed to prove themselves in battle in order to equal or surpass predecessors in military exploits. Gods ran before the kings and struck down enemies in battle when the king laid claim to personal tutelary deities. On occasion, kings engaged in hand-to-hand fighting with enemies. While no kings were killed in action, one of the early kings may have died from battle wounds. Members of the royal family held the highest ranks in the army and none were full-time soldiers. Many nobles who owned rural estates joined kings on military campaigns on a seasonal basis. Serving in the army led to land, booty in the form of cattle, and prisoners of war who worked on rural estates helping to grow crops, tend orchards or raise livestock. Career soldiers served at the lower levels, were always on duty, and were quartered in Hattusa. The king stipulated that none of the recruits could be slaves and no substitutions were allowed through bribery. Recruits from the same region bunked together since they could share a common language.

Kings were accountable to the Storm God; as the steward of the Storm God, the king made sure that the land that belonged to the deity was in the hands of those the king picked, with divine guidance, as vassal rulers. The image of the king hovered somewhere between heaven and earth; during the Festival of Enthronement he wore royal vestments, was anointed with fragrant oil, and then formally given his throne name. In extant reliefs, he is generally depicted wearing a skull cap and a long ankle-length robe, symbolizing his office as the high priest of the Hittite world. He carried a curved staff as a symbol of judiciary power. His subjects were equally shut out from the outside in the acropolis known as Buyukkale (big castle). Key posts were held by sons for diplomatic missions abroad, especially to viceregal kingdoms of Carchemish and Aleppo.

Those in service to the king included the Gal Mesedi, who was chief bodyguard, considered to be the most prestigious jobs. It was often given to the king's brother or close member of the family. The Mesedi formed an elite guard armed with spears and their mission was to protect the king. They have been compared to the praetorian guard of imperial Rome, the personal bodyguards of Caesar, except fewer in numbers and often only assembling in groups of 12 at any one time. They shared their duties with the gold spearmen, which ensured loyalty toward one another. Another prominent figure was the Gal Gestin, or chief of the wine stewards, who was in charge of military commands. An interesting historical document called the 'Bel Madgalti text" contains a job description for one of the most crucial jobs, that of the Bel Madgalti or "auriyas ishas" in Hittite, who was the lord of the watchtower or the king's district governor. The document reviews strict instructions that ensure that the fortresses and towns were securely locked and included other management duties of the king's lands and instructions for presiding over local judiciaries. Scribes translated all Hittite documents and advised the king. The present was firmly rooted in the past, because every decision was based on the past and archives were regularly consulted.

Rank, status, and pecking order were important in the Bronze Age world. Even a son of the second rank did not inspire the same respect as a first-rank son. Palace servants, cup-bearers, table-men, cooks, heralds, stableboys, captains of thousands, and any members of the royal court shared a status and sense of superiority based on their service to the king. Success in diplomacy depended on royal princes and high-level officials with status-conscious foreign kings and vassals.

Everything served the interest of the king since it was a centralized palace economy. However, the king was also very hands-on in the community. They appeared as principal celebrants in a demanding round of religious festivals all year long that sometimes took them on pilgrimages to main religious centers of the kingdom. Life was highly regulated. Farmers, craftsmen, and soldiers worked to benefit the state. The chief source of revenue for the state was from agricultural surplus taxes (a percentage was determined of one's produce), as well as tributes and booty from military campaigns. Women were priestesses of high status and musicians and took part in festival activities. They also took part in rituals in many capacities. Wise women operated in concert with practitioners like physicians, diviners, augurs, and other parts of society. The higher-status women escaped being classified as property. Queens even issued edicts and cosigned international treaties with their husbands. In religious circles, literate women composed the texts of many rituals. However, the majority of Hittite women were wives and mothers. Kings usually had one queen, but also had a harem. Poor women worked as millers, bakers, cooks, weavers, fullers, clothes makers, tavern keepers, midwives and physicians. There are many powerful royal women whose careers are covered in Hittite history, including Queen Puduhelpa, wife of King Hattusili III, who took a hand in law and diplomacy. She even had her own independent seal and a joint seal with her husband. Her seal appears on one of the most historical documents that the world has preserved: the peace treaty between Egypt and the Hittites, which will be discussed further.

Here are some of the most notable kings and their achievements. Hattusili I made Hattusa the capital, conquered large areas of Anatolia, and campaigned in northern Syria and across the Euphrates between 1650-1620 BCE. Between 1620-1590 BCE, his grandson Mursili I conquered Aleppo and Babylon. Mursili I was assassinated and enemies invaded between 1590-1525 BCE, after which Telupinu seized the throne and regained some of the lost territories. Between 1500-1400 BCE, the Kingdom of Mitanni emerged. The Hittite New Kingdom reasserted authority as an international power between 1400-1350 BCE with military campaigns in Anatolia and

Syria. Hattusa was abandoned. Between 1350-1322 BCE, Tudhaliya III and his son Suppiluliuma I regained the kingdom. These early years were characterized by profound military crisis, but Tudhaliya turned things around. Excavators have found a cache of seal impressions and clay tablets dated during his reign that include land-grants, inventories of goods, personnel matters and matters for oracular consultations.

Suppiluliuma I became the king of kings for the Hittites and would be known as the most memorable Hittite ruler. He destroyed Mitanni by 1320 BCE and conducted military campaigns in Syria and Mesopotamia. He established viceregal kingdoms at Aleppo and Carchemish in Syria. He controlled the most powerful empire in the 14th and 13th centuries BCE. The most dramatic expansion of Hittite power took place under his reign, despite the fact that Egypt maintained its dominance over the disputed Canaan region after Pharaoh Seti (r. 1308-1291 BCE) invaded Canaan against the Bedouins and the Hittites. During his rule, the Egyptian requested king in a letter that the Arzawan ruler send him a princess to marry, which resulted in an international alliance. The reason for the marriage and resulting alliance was most likely related to the rise of the Hittite empire under Suppiluliuma and the threat that Hatti posed to the Egyptian territories in the north. The alliance assured Egypt of Arzawa's loyalty and helped slow the Hittites. Arzawa ended up being defeated by Suppiluliuma anyway and split into three vassal kingdoms (the Kingdom of Mira with Kuwaliya, the Seha River Land, and Hapalla) around 1300 BCE.

During his reign, Suppiluliuma secured sworn pacts between kings and had regular exchanges of letters in the elite highly exclusive club that he and the kings of Egypt, Babylon, and Assyria formed. He secured the Egyptian-controlled territory of Amka, but the prisoners of war who were brought back to Hattusa introduced a deadly plague into Hatti that ended up claiming the king and his son. Chaos unfolded when he died, since he didn't have time to consolidate his conquests. The subjugated regions threw off the Hittite rule under his son Mursili II.

Infamously, Mursili's son Muwatalli (r. 1295-1272 BCE) confronted Rameses II in the famous battle of Qadesh circa 1274. Kadesh (or Qadesh), an ancient city of the Levant in the 15th century BCE, and competition for control over this region, lay at the center of the hostilities between Egypt and the Hittites. The international system circa 1500-1250 BCE involving Egypt, Babylon, Assyria and the Hittites marked an era of considerable warfare, especially for control of the Canaanite states, but also in terms of international trade routes and political ambitions. Thousands of Egyptian and Hittite troops faced off in one of the great chariot wars. It is one of the most documented military engagements of ancient times. Muwatalli captured Kadesh, and the city remained loyal to the Hittite kings until the collapse of the empire at the end of the Bronze Age. According to historian Gregorio Zaide in "World History," the Hittites foiled Egypt's attempt to conquer Syria by checking the invading forces of Rameses II. Kadesh was a strategically important city in northern Syria.

Hittite prosperity was very dependent on control of trade routes and metal sources. Since Northern Syria was an important and vital route linking the Cilician Gates to Mesopotamia, it was important for controlling trade in the Levant and southern Syria. Neither were outright winners since the battle results were inconclusive, although the historical record has been falsified in an effort for propaganda depending on whether you read the Hittite or Egyptian version of the battle. It is considered the largest chariot battle ever fought. They settled their differences and divided control of the Syria-Palestine region, with Egypt dominating the southern coastal region and Hatti controlling the inland and northernmost coast as far south as Beqa. Muwatalli also added Wilusa (Troy) as a vassal.

The Treaty of Kadesh was signed in 1258 BCE under King Hattusili III, Muwatalli's successor. It is considered one of the oldest completely surviving fully preserved international treaties in history and fixed the mutual boundaries in Canaan. It is also the earliest fully preserved international treaty between two of the most important empires of the Late Bronze Age. The cuneiform tablet is recorded in the Akkadian language. The friendly relations between the two kings were further strengthened by the marriage of a daughter of Hattusili II with Rameses II. They also exchanged diplomatic gifts. In many ways, the Battle of Kadesh ushered in peace and stability, which brought trade and economic growth.

Culture

The Hittite civilization was a highly derivative one and there was considerable influence of the Near Eastern world on the civilization of Greece. Similarities and parallels can be found between Hittite and Greek traditions and customs, as illustrated by literary and mythological motifs, ritual practices and methods of communicating with gods. They generally wrote in Akkadian when dealing outside of Anatolia. They had numerous rock reliefs that were widely distributed, located from the Aegean to the upper Euphrates River. Their centralized character in Hittite art was demonstrated by the sharing of the same motifs between reliefs and, on a far smaller scale, seals and jewelry. Generally, they didn't have art for art's sake; everything was used to employ the needs of the entire system.

Most of their writing was prose, but that could be a result of how unsuitable cuneiform was to rendering the language they used. They did however enjoy music gatherings and songs. Their mythology narratives explain the cosmic order and are embedded in rituals – Moon that Fell From Heaven, Vanishing God or Telipinu Myth, and Illuyanka or the Combat of the Storm God with the Dragon, to name a few. In the latter narrative, the Storm God relied on a human helper. Some of the myths told of the topography of the netherworld. Mythologies of foreign origin like 'The Epic of Gilgamesh' were found in the Hittite Capital's library translated into Hurrian and Hittite, with some details altered in the Hittite language rendered to suit their conceptions and interests. According to Gary Beckman, it was imported solely for scribal instructions. Their literature ranged from folkloric motifs and humorous narratives for the purpose of moral and political lessons to mockeries and narratives concerning kings' campaigns compared to other Near East kings. The tablets included deeds, royal edicts, treaties, hymns and pleas, wisdom literature, similes and anecdotal texts.

The Hittites were fond of recreational activities. At their religious festivals, they held athletic contests and feats of strength after the ritual banquet and before a sacred procession. They staged mock combat representing the divine battle symbolizing good and evil. They held archery contests in the presence of the king where the winner received wine and the loser suffered humiliation of stripping naked and bringing water for the others. They held weightlifting contests where youth attempted to move large stones and lift heavy weights. They also threw stones (shot putting) to entertain the gods and received animals as prizes. Some artwork depicted bull leaping, wrestling and boxing, although the evidence is considered fragmentary. The king's bodyguards competed in foot races for the title of "marshal" or "holder of the king's chariot reins." They participated in dance, acrobatics, hunting, and are considered by some researchers as a forerunner for the Greek concept of competition or agon, where winning was paramount.

Gods Among Them

The Hittites were polytheistic. Their principal god was the Storm God (or Weather God) who held a position like Zeus among the Greeks. In the Kumarbi myth, the Storm God Tesub is the chief deity in their religious system. When he appeared in texts, he was associated with aspects of nature and in politics as the head of each entity or settlement. The sacred animal of the Storm God was the bull, since it was a symbol of virility and possessed a loud voice. In the hierarchy of gods, the mother goddess came before the spouse of the Storm God. The Hittite Sun Goddess was Arinna. The universe of the Hittites was an integrated system; under the right circumstances, gods might mingle with humans. As mentioned, humans served gods and gods were dependent on humans. Satisfied deities would cause crops to thrive and society to prosper. An offended god or goddess could wreak havoc both personally and communally. The Hittites would take corrective measures whenever they figured out which deity they had angered.

They had a very complicated religion; it is difficult to pin down the exact number of gods and goddesses they worshipped, but records indicate there were a little over 600. Lists of deities were summoned to witness treaties. The treaty between the king of Amurru and the Hittite king Mursili II included 20 different deities. The treaty between king Hukkana of Hayasa-Azzi (eastern Anatolia) and king Suppiluliuma I likewise contained over 20 gods. Texts with religious content constituted a large part of the clay tablets discovered. Their divine community increased continuously to include deities from raided territories, as the Hittites absorbed and assimilated these gods within the fabric of their own culture. They lacked an official religious doctrine or dogma.

Among the Empires

The archaeology of the Hittites revolves around imperialism: there are edifices devoted to defense and control and symbols of power and persuasion. The Hittites, among the other eastern Mediterranean empires, became affluent during the Bronze Age, based on a booming international trade where they and the Egyptians played key roles. Other powerful states of the time included the Assyrians, Hurrians, Babylonians, Mycenaeans and Elamites, all of which had to deal with the Hittites in times of war and peace. These interrelations were too extensive to cover here; however it is worth noting that the Hittites handled their foreign affairs in a sophisticated manner. They were known to use trade embargoes as a weapon against the attacking Mycenaeans in places. The Hittites referred to their region as Ahhiyawa.

There is archaeological evidence of land deeds, art, seal impressions, correspondences between foreign "brothers" (kings) and their local viceregal authorities that the Hittites entrusted in regions that had been conquered and then pledged fealty to the Hittites. The expansion and contraction of the Hittite empire is well-documented. They were definitely movers and shakers and took cultural pride in advancing the Hittite Empire with an exceptional practice of conducting treaties under a system that shows some examples of limited democracy, given their development of diplomatic and bureaucratic bodies. Power rested across a complex web of parochial townships and villages under a collective governance, but nonetheless, despite a centralized authority under a king, their council of elders and nobility did not forfeit power to the absolute control of the king, despite the absence of elections.

Collapse

Between 1200-1150 BCE, many states collapsed as both foreign and domestic problems devastated the empire. The mysterious Sea Peoples attacked on land and on sea in the southern coastal region. There was international strife. The Assyrians defeated the Hittites in 1237-1209 BCE in a battle in northern Mesopotamia as the kingdom was in decline. During the reign of their last attested king Suppiluliuma II, the Hittites engaged in naval warfare off the coast of Cyprus for the first known time in their history. Internal upheavals, including conflicts within the royal family concerning the legitimacy of the king, pressure from the Kashka people in northern Anatolia, and crop failures and famine were all exacerbated by increasing climate change. The struggle between the Hattusili and Mursili lines dominated the final decade of the empire. They were not flexible enough to react quickly to change and their palace economy collapsed.

The exact circumstances of the fall of the vast Hittite Empire are debated, but many of these factors are seen as contributory. The Kaska people played the role of unconquerable frontier barbarians from the 15th century to the end of the empire. The Kaska had no kings, making it impossible for the Hittites to make treaties with them. The Kaska also had no wealth to seize. Despite Hittite efforts, they were a major force to reckon with. Some records reveal that the Egyptians say that the Sea Peoples destroyed the Hittites before moving on to raid Egypt. Attacks by the Sea People also disrupted trade for the Phoenicians, Mycenaeans, Hittites and Egyptians.

In fact, current research published in New Scientist supports the theory that the lost civilization of Sea Peoples may have sparked the first world war 3,000 years ago, helping experts explain how the empires of the time (the Egyptian New Kingdom, the Hittites of central Anatolia, and the Mycenaeans of mainland Greece) that had otherwise been in coexistence all rapidly declined around the same time. It may have happened about 3,200 years prior to the first world war, an event that archaeologist Eberhard Zangger has dubbed "World War Zero." The theory is leading to further examination. Zangger is not the only one who is still trying to piece things together. Professor Eric Cline, director of the Capitol Archaeological Institute at George Washington University, suggests that the interconnectedness of these great societies meant that the collapse of one also affected the others and that the Late Bronze Age civilizations were not able to weather the storm facing all the factors that happened in quick succession. He thinks the Sea People have been unfairly blamed for causing the collapse of these great civilizations and although they were definitely a menace, there were greater forces at work. He considers their demise a warning. Since similarly-intertwined civilizations collapsed just after 1200 BCE, it should be a warning that if it happened once, it can happen again; some of the modern day equivalents of the Sea People in the form of the chaos in Libya, Syria, Egypt and Iraq mirror some of the same situations at the end of the Bronze Age.

Chapter Five

Notable Achievements, Ongoing Exploration and Unraveling their Extraordinary Mysteries

What thanks do we owe the Hittites? For one thing, they preserved the records of the times meticulously and are the bridge between the East and Semitic world. Thanks to their tradition-preserving culture of scribes, they saved the records of Babylon's cosmology. They innovated the use of the horse-drawn chariot in warfare; their two-wheeled chariot systems were lighter, making them highly maneuverable with the axle set forward for stability. These are considered the inventors of some of the first effective siege engines, as the rider could free their arms for using a weapon while riding. The texts that they preserved contain some of the earliest written records of Sanskrit, Greek, Latin, Indo-European and other languages. They reared horses like many Indo-Europeans did traditionally, but their approach to training horses influenced many other cultures. Scholars have found that many of the ideas, problems, and thoughts from Greece may have originated in Oriental thinking, including Hittite thought, and research continues to see whether some of it can be interpreted as precursors to Homer.

Finally, as mentioned they were the first nation to advance and utilize iron in making tools and weapons which were then transferred to the civilized nations of the world. The ongoing warfare of this period of history allowed for humankind to refine social structures and armies that produced every weapon that was developed for the next three thousand years until the introduction of gunpowder. The discovery and use of iron marked a dramatic increase in the frequency of war and heralded advances in military operational ability, strategies, and training.

As we consider the current findings, studies about the Hittites keep attempting to unravel the biggest mysteries that are still left unanswered. In 2007, by studying the time period when the Hittites sacked Symra, which is also associated with a mysterious plague according to associated methods, Italian molecular biologist Dr. Diro Trevisanato found that the Hittites had mastered the art of biological warfare; they introduced infected sheep into cities they wanted to conquer. These sheep carried rabbit fever, which has no known vaccine. In 2013, archaeologists in suburban Istanbul found that the early Hittites ventured into Europe, even though it had previously been thought that they had remained in Asia. They found iron Hittite god and goddess statues, bitumen, tin and ceramic pieces which offer the first proof that they entered Europe. In 2015, a chef developed a unique way to study the ancient civilization: its cuisine. Using information gleaned from ancient tablets found in Alacahöyük, chef Ömür Akkor, along with Aykut Çinaroğlu, professor of archaeology at Ankara University, prepared a meal that might have appeared on Hittite tables 4,000 years ago. In 2015, 15 ancient species of Hittite trees were planted in one of the most important centers of the Hittite civilization in the central Anatolian province of Corum. The project will be finished by 2017.

Also in 2015, an excavation at the Central Anatolian province in Corum unearthed various artifacts in a 3,700-year-old mine factory with smooth and durable walls and a capacity of 4,000 people. A water channel, was also discovered, showcasing the importance the Hittites attached to hygiene. The team believed they would continue to reveal new artifacts that would surprise the archaeological world. In 2016, the Koç University's Research Center for Anatolian Civilizations opened an exhibition named "Scent and the City" which asked visitors to discover four millennia of civilizations through their noses. The scents were drawn from literature, traditions, rituals and the economy from the Hittite to ancient Greek and Roman civilizations to the Byzantine and Ottoman empires.

The mysteries of the Hittites continue to unravel.

Conclusion

As scholars, historians and archaeologists fill in the holes about the Hittites, we will witness the complexity of their thinking, their lives and the impact they have had on our own. We continue to be enthralled when we learn how they were more relatable than many of the previous civilizations, having developed moral insights, the power of analysis, sensitivity and ethical behavior as they fought to bring their empire to preeminence in the region surrounded by competing Near East powers. We can continue to gain an understanding of the connection between the Hittites and Troy and develop a further appreciation of their development of trade links, inter-dependence, and astuteness in the spirit of international cooperation as a cradle of human culture. Their ideas in search of common humanity during their campaigns to impose Hittite power in the lands of the Near East can help us understand empire-building in the past, present and future. There are still so many fascinating questions to ask and answers to find. How did the Hittites influence Greece and philosophy? What do we make of their precedents in their technical, political and humane endeavors? These answers and so many more questions lie ahead in the continual exploration of the Hittites.

Made in United States
North Haven, CT
08 August 2024

55820576R00024